In Celebration

Date

Guests

Name

Thoughts

Name

Guests

Thoughts

Guests

Name

_____

_____

_____

Thoughts

_____

_____

_____

_____

_____

_____

_____

_____

_____

_____

_____

Guests

Name

Thoughts

Name

Guests

Thoughts

Guests

Name

Thoughts

Guests

Name

Thoughts

Guests

Name

Thoughts

Guests

Name

Thoughts

_____

_____

_____

_____

_____

_____

_____

_____

_____

_____

_____

Guests

Name

Thoughts

Guests

Name

Thoughts

_____

_____

_____

_____

_____

_____

_____

_____

_____

_____

_____

_____

_____

_____

Guests

Name

Thoughts

_____

_____

_____

_____

_____

_____

_____

_____

_____

_____

_____

_____

_____

_____

_____

Guests

Name

Thoughts

Guests

Name

Thoughts

_____

_____

_____

_____

_____

_____

_____

_____

_____

_____

_____

Guests

Name

Thoughts

Guests

Name

Thoughts

_____

_____

_____

_____

_____

_____

_____

_____

_____

_____

_____

_____

Guests

Name

_____

_____

_____

_____

Thoughts

_____

_____

_____

_____

_____

_____

_____

_____

_____

_____

_____

Guests

Name

Thoughts

Guests

Name

_____

_____

_____

_____

Thoughts

_____

_____

_____

_____

_____

_____

_____

_____

_____

_____

_____

Guests

Name

Thoughts

Guests

Name

Thoughts

_____

_____

_____

_____

_____

_____

_____

_____

_____

_____

_____

_____

Guests

Name

Thoughts

_____

_____

_____

_____

_____

_____

_____

_____

_____

_____

_____

_____

_____

_____

Guests

Name

_____

_____

_____

Thoughts

_____

_____

_____

_____

_____

_____

_____

_____

_____

_____

_____

Guests

Name

Thoughts

Guests

Name

Thoughts

_____

_____

_____

_____

_____

_____

_____

_____

_____

_____

_____

Guests

Name

Thoughts

Guests

Name

Thoughts

_____

_____
_____
_____
_____

_____
_____
_____
_____

_____
_____
_____

Guests

Name

Thoughts

Guests

Name

Thoughts

_____

_____
_____
_____
_____

_____

_____

_____
_____
_____

_____
_____
_____

Guests

Name

Thoughts

_____

_____

_____

_____

_____

_____

_____

_____

_____

_____

_____

_____

Guests

Name

Thoughts

Guests

Name

Thoughts

_____

_____

_____

_____

_____

_____

_____

_____

_____

_____

_____

_____

_____

_____

_____

Guests

Name

Thoughts

Guests

Name

_____

_____

_____

Thoughts

_____

_____

_____

_____

_____

_____

_____

_____

_____

_____

_____

Guests

Name

Thoughts

Name

Guests

Thoughts

_____

_____

_____

_____

_____

_____

_____

_____

_____

_____

_____

_____

_____

_____

_____

_____

Guests

Name

Thoughts

Guests

Name

Thoughts

Guests

Name

Thoughts

Guests

Name

Thoughts

_____

_____
_____
_____
_____

_____

_____
_____
_____
_____

_____

Name

Guests

Thoughts

Guests

Name

Thoughts

_____

_____

_____

_____

_____

_____

_____

_____

_____

_____

_____

_____

_____

Guests

Name

Thoughts

Guests

Name

Thoughts

_____

_____

_____

_____

_____

_____

_____

_____

_____

_____

_____

_____

Guests

Name

Thoughts

_____

_____

_____

_____

_____

_____

_____

_____

_____

_____

_____

Guests

Name

Thoughts

Guests

Name

Thoughts

_____

_____

_____

_____

_____

_____

_____

_____

_____

_____

_____

_____

_____

_____

Guests

Name

Thoughts

Guests

Name

Thoughts

Guests

Name

Thoughts

_____   _____
_____
_____
_____
_____
_____
_____   _____
_____
_____
_____
_____   _____
_____
_____

Guests

Name

Thoughts

Guests

Name

Thoughts

_____ _____

_____

_____

_____

_____ _____

_____

_____

_____ _____

_____

_____

Guests

Name

Thoughts

Name

Guests

Thoughts

Guests

Name

Thoughts

Guests

Name

Thoughts

Guests

Name

Thoughts

Guests

Name

Thoughts

_____

_____
_____
_____
_____
_____
_____
_____
_____
_____
_____
_____
_____
_____
_____

Guests

Name

Thoughts

_____

_____
_____
_____
_____
_____

_____

_____
_____
_____
_____
_____

_____

_____
_____
_____
_____

Name

Guests

Thoughts

_____

_____

_____

_____

_____

_____

_____

_____

_____

_____

_____

_____

Guests

Name

_____

_____

_____

Thoughts

_____

_____

_____

_____

_____

_____

_____

_____

_____

- - - - - - - - - - - - - - - - - -

Guests

Name

Thoughts

Guests

Name

Thoughts

Guests

Name

Thoughts

Guests

Name

_____

_____

Thoughts

_____
_____
_____
_____
_____
_____
_____
_____
_____
_____
_____
_____
_____

Guests

Name

_____

_____

_____

Thoughts

_____

_____

_____

_____

_____

_____

_____

_____

_____

_____

_____

_____

Guests

Name

Thoughts

Guests

Name

_____

_____

_____

Thoughts

_____

_____

_____

_____

_____

_____

_____

_____

_____

_____

_____

_____

Guests

Name

Thoughts

_____

_____

_____

_____

_____

_____

_____

_____

_____

_____

_____

_____

Guests

Name

Thoughts

Guests

Name

Thoughts

_____

_____

_____

_____

_____

_____

_____

_____

_____

_____

_____

_____

Guests

Name

Thoughts

Guests

Name

Thoughts

Guests

Name

Thoughts

Guests

Name

_____

_____

_____

_____

Thoughts

_____

_____

_____

_____

_____

_____

_____

_____

_____

_____

_____

Guests

Name

Thoughts

Name

Guests

Thoughts

_____

_____

_____

_____

_____

_____

_____

_____

_____

_____

_____

_____

_____

_____

Guests

Name

Thoughts

_____

_____

_____

_____

_____

_____

_____

_____

_____

_____

_____

_____

_____

Guests

Name

Thoughts

Name

Guests

Thoughts

_____

_____

_____

_____

_____

_____

_____

_____

_____

_____

_____

_____

_____

_____

_____

Guests

Name

Thoughts

Guests

Name

Thoughts

Guests

Name

Thoughts

Name

Guests

Thoughts

_____

_____

_____

Guests

Name

Thoughts

Guests

Name

Thoughts

_____

_____

Guests

Name

Thoughts

_____

_____

_____

_____

_____

_____

_____

_____

_____

_____

_____

_____

_____

Guests

Name

Thoughts

_____

_____
_____
_____
_____
_____
_____
_____

_____

_____
_____
_____
_____
_____
_____

_____

_____
_____
_____

Guests

Name

Thoughts

Guests

Name

Thoughts

Guests

Name

Thoughts

Guests

Name

_____

_____

_____

Thoughts

_____

_____

_____

_____

_____

_____

_____

_____

_____

_____

_____

_____

Guests

Name

Thoughts

Guests

Name

Thoughts

_____

_____

_____

_____

_____

_____

_____

_____

_____

_____

_____

_____

_____

_____

_____

_____

Guests

Name

Thoughts

_____

_____

_____

_____

_____

_____

_____

_____

_____

_____

_____

_____

_____

_____

Guests

Name

Thoughts

_____

_____

_____

_____

_____

_____

_____

_____

_____

_____

_____

_____

_____

Guests

Name

_____

_____

_____

_____

Thoughts

_____

_____

_____

_____

_____

_____

_____

_____

_____

_____

_____

_____

Guests

Name

Thoughts

_____

_____

_____

_____

_____

_____

_____

_____

_____

_____

_____

_____

_____

_____

Guests

Name

Thoughts

_____

_____

_____

_____

_____

_____

_____

_____

_____

_____

_____

_____

_____

_____

Guests

Name

Thoughts

_____

_____

_____

_____

_____

_____

_____

_____

_____

_____

_____

_____

_____

_____

_____

Guests

Name

_____

_____

Thoughts

_____
_____
_____
_____
_____
_____
_____
_____
_____
_____
_____
_____
_____

Guests

Name

_____

_____

_____

Thoughts

_____

_____

_____

_____

_____

_____

_____

_____

_____

_____

_____

_____

_____

Guests

Name

Thoughts

_____

_____

_____

_____

_____

_____

_____

_____

_____

_____

_____

Guests

Name

Thoughts

_____

_____

_____

_____

_____

_____

_____

_____

_____

_____

_____

_____

_____

_____

_____

Guests

Name

Thoughts

_____

_____

_____

_____

_____

_____

_____

_____

_____

_____

_____

_____

_____

_____

_____

_____

Guests

Name

Thoughts

_____

_____

_____

_____

_____

_____

_____

_____

_____

_____

_____

_____

Guests

Name

Thoughts

_____

_____

_____

_____

_____

_____

_____

_____

_____

_____

_____

_____

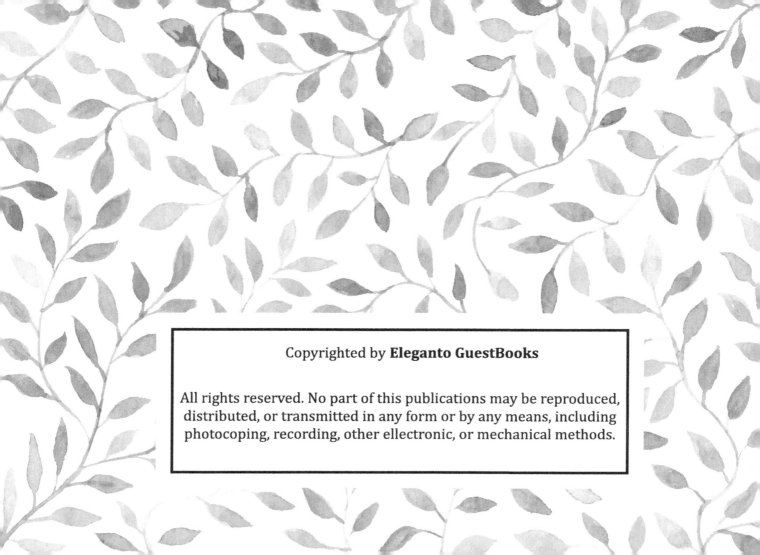

Made in the USA
Coppell, TX
26 April 2024

31741025R00063